CONTENTS

About The Author

Alistair Gray is the Founder and Managing Director of Renaissance & Company and one of Europe's leading strategic management consultants. He is also a lecturer on strategic management on the MBA programme at Strathclyde Business School and Masters programme at Loughborough University London as well as Visiting Professor at the University of Strathclyde's Design Manufacturing and Engineering Management. He is Senior Independent Director at Silence Therapeutics PLC, a biopharma business and Chair of Scottish Enterprise's Pension Scheme's Trustee Board.

1. Introduction

2019 was a special year in my relationship with BrewDog.

I had, of course, been familiar with them as a business, probably through their use of crowdfunding and some of their promotional 'stunts'.

In 2019, I had the pleasure and privilege to work with the boards and executives of Opportunity North East to facilitate the creation of a vision of success for 2030. Opportunity North East was launched in December 2015, following extensive consultation with the region's business community and discussion with the public sector. It is the private sector's response to the special economic challenges in the region, especially in light of the potentially negative impact of the decline of the oil and gas exploration industry.

There are few examples beyond the John Wood Group PLC of genuinely global companies.. In 2019 BrewDog were a shining light in the north east and Speyside, a region already home to a number of successful food and drink companies such as Baxters of Fochabers and Walkers of Aberlour as well as a good number of whisky distillers, notably Edrington (The Macallan) and William Grant (Glenfiddich and Balvenie).

In 2019 I also led the Strategy Consulting in Practice module for the MBA 25 class at Strathclyde Business School. One of the students in the class was a senior employee of BrewDog and my curiosity was increased hearing her describe the special working environment and community that had been created in the company's first decade of operation.

Routledge, my publishers delivered The Game Changer to the shelves of booksellers in 2019. In assembling the book, I concluded that organisations in business and sport who had not only improved performance – they had changed the game in their industry or sector – they displayed 5 key features. In these real-life examples the Game Changers:

1. Broke the rules – they challenged existing paradigms
2. Worked it out themselves – they embraced change management
3. Planned for a step-change in performance
4. Changed organizational performance
5. Leaders at all levels in the organisation championed the change.

The difference with the real Game Changers lies in their ambition and capability to address and execute the 5 features, all at the same time, through a major change initiative.

In this little book I address what I believe lies behind BrewDog's performance and conclude, at the end, the extent to which they are surfing a wave or truly changing the game in the craft beer industry.

I hope it proves to be a useful book that will inspire others to follow BrewDog's example - to start a small craft brewery in a remote part of Scotland, distant from key markets to create a global leader in a new segment of their industry.

In 2019 I also became an Equity Punk with a modest investment as a shareholder.

Alistair Gray, Glasgow 2020

2. Brewdog Breaks The Rules Of The Beer Game

Fifteen *years ago, James Watt was fishing for mackerel and halibut on a commercial trawler off the north east coast of Scotland. He had a dog, a modest pay-check, and few prospects in a region in post-oil boom decline. Today, Watt is worth $337 million and travels the world leading and managing one of the fastest-growing ventures in the UK. Together with Martin Dickie they have changed the game of the brewing industry, as a response to the generic brands that dominated the UK market, to become the epicentre of the UK craft beer industry. Their's is a story of courage, passion and love.* I will endeavour, in this little book, *to do justice to their achievements and evidence their status as true Game Changers.*

In the Beginning

Former law graduate James Watt, turned brewer, did not make his fortune as a tech entrepreneur or a securities trader. He and his business partner, Martin Dickie, produce craft beer. Their company, BrewDog is known for its zesty "punk" ales and over-the-top publicity stunts. The two founders once drove a World War II-era tank through the City of London waving banners displaying their company logo (a yelping dog) they produced the world's strongest beer. BrewDog was born with missionary zeal – "to revolutionise the beer industry and completely redefine beer-drinking culture. We're determined to make a stand for independence, a stand for quality and stand for craft. And a big part of this is shamelessly spreading our passion for great craft beer." Seen by the established beer industry as idiosyncratic they have achieved leadership in the UK craft beer industry in less than 10 years through their passion, innovation and entrepreneurship that is the envy of many. Far from targeting a gap in the beer market they relentlessly created a new market with a new generation of consumers.

They initially filled bottles by hand, sold their brews at farmers' markets, and blew their savings. The pair had a chance meeting with Michael Jackson, the leading author of many influential books on beer and whisky, that helped define the opportunity, so aligned was Jackson to their vision. Then in 2008 the two 24-year-olds made a breakthrough when their beers took first place in a contest sponsored by Tesco, Britain's biggest supermarket chain. Told they had just won shelf space for 2,000 cases a week, Watt did not blink and promised to deliver. The pair wrangled a £20,000 loan out of HSBC, bought some equipment, and dubbed their flagship offering Punk IPA. They vowed to fight the "insipid, artificially flavoured offerings" of corporates such as Anhauser Busch and Heineken. Everything BrewDog does is about the beer.

"We want to make people as passionate about great beer as

*we are. Change perceptions, challenge conventions, but do it
on our terms. We've always said we'll either succeed, or be
some massive great crash-and-burn failure. But that's fine,
because the space in between is really fucking boring."*
James Watt 2019

In 2018 BrewDog was valued at £1.7bn ($2.2bn) after its latest crowd-funding round and the 2017 sale of a 23 percent stake to a U.S. private equity firm. Its revenue soared 60 percent in 2018, to about £179m, as it notched another year of net profits. BrewDog has created more than 1,200 jobs in the Britain, sells beer in 60 countries and owns more than 90 bars and restaurants in the UK. Profits have been reinvested in the business over the years and now at scale operating in many of the best (not necessarily the largest) beer markets in the world, the company is well placed for growth in its value. London is the epicentre of UK Craft beer and 'googling' Brewdog places it in the top 5 beer companies in the world. Yet its largest competitor is 2500 times their size. In 2019 turnover grew a further 55% and their case sales passed a landmark 1m in the US with distribution extended from 9 states planning to 15. They now have over 50 franchises globally – without initially realising what the concept meant.

Catching the Wave

BrewDog caught the market just as younger drinkers were discovering the bracing tropical-tinged flavours that turned American craft beer pioneers such as Sierra Nevada Brewing Company and Boston Beer Company, the maker of Sam
Adams, into industry-changing forces worth billions of dollars.

But what truly propelled the company was its unique 'gonzo' market-ing. To claim the title of world's strongest beer from a German brewer, Watt and Dickie made Sink the Bismarck, a "quadruple IPA" with an al-cohol-by-volume level of 41%. And they projected 60-foot-high naked images of themselves onto the Houses of Parliament to trumpet their plan to "take the craft beer revolution to the next level" (a BrewDog sign covered their private parts). Even stunts that failed (like Pink IPA) hit the mark for their equity punks, and increased the adoration of the brand.

Last year the company opened a hotel next to its Ohio brewery called the DogHouse that features taps in its 32 rooms, beer-infused soaps, and even well-stocked brew fridges in the bathrooms. "They've created this elusive brand equity that's based on more than enjoying their beer," says Spiros Malandrakis, a beverage industry analyst with market researcher Euromonitor International. "With BrewDog, you can drink a beer in the shower at their hotel."

BrewDog's strong branding was a big reason why TSG Consumer Partners (a San Francisco-based private equity firm that's pumped money into consumer-focused brands including Famous Amos, Vitaminwater, and Planet Fitness) invested £100m in the company in April 2017. Despite his uber-cool public image, Watt is steeped in the details of his business. His office suite features a replica of the beer shelf at a nearby Tesco supermarket so he can evaluate how the labels on his products stand out next to those of rivals. Still, he says, BrewDog remains true to its artisanal roots and will never sell out to a big brewer. "For us, the bigger companies are responsible for the bastardisation and commoditisation of beer, which is everything we're against," he says. Asked how he squares that with the TSG deal, Watt points out that iconic U.S. players such as Southern California's Stone Brewing Co.

have also tapped buyout funds. "That just helps us compete without having to sell our souls."

Bring in the Crowd

With big investors few and far between, the start-up turned to the nascent crowd-funding market as a way to raise capital. In 2009, it launched its first crowd-funding drive, dubbed Equity for Punks after its signature Punk IPA, and attracted more than 1,300 investors. Its anti-business model was born. The offering was a success and the initiative raised £7.5m through the first three issues. A fourth round of fund-raising aiming to raise £25m is currently underway and has already raised £6m.

An early user of crowd-funding, BrewDog raised £67 million from almost 120,000 "equity punks" and leap-frogged chains to open their own bars and expand their global business.

The AGMs (Annual General Meetings of the Equity Punks) are held in major UK conference centres and in the US take the form of a pop concert. 7000 attended the event in Winchester, Ohio with the first European AGM held in Berlin in September 2019. 15,000 attended the 2019 event in Aberdeen. In 2020, during COVID19 LOCKDOWN

The offering was used to fund ambitious expansion plans unveiled at its alternative take on the AGM, which included music from rock band Idlewild and beer tasting. The expansion plans are more mainstream and include new bars, a distillery and brewery expansion, such as a new state-of-the-art craft brewery on a new site in Ohio.

The brewer is taking its craft beer – product and community - to the US, having provisionally agreed a deal to build a new 100,000 sq.ft brewery in Columbus, Ohio. In addition to the 100-barrel brew house, the 42 acres of land will house BrewDog's US offices, a visitor centre, a craft beer restaurant and a taproom. Once opened, BrewDog will be brewing its full line-up of beers as well as small batch special brews unique to the US brewery.

In this next chapter we examine the key strategic management activities carried out in real time and in the third part compare BrewDog against the 5 features of The Game Changers.

3. Brewdog - The 21St Century Kwik-Fit?

I t is interesting to draw parallels between BrewDog and Kwik-Fit and to further understand the rise and rise of the craft brewer and disrupter, without suggesting that the two enterprises were the same. When writing the Game Changer I persuaded Sir Tom Farmer, the great entrepreneur and founder of Kwik-Fit to contribute the foreword to the book. During our conversations he outlined what underpinned KwikFit's disruption of the traditional tyre and exhaust business in the 1970's.

I examined a number of the key management functions that underpin the success of their businesses to date e.g. strategic management, engagement with stakeholders, marketing and enabling their people to fulfil their potential.

Although there are significant differences between them, the more I understood the philosophy and principles behind BrewDog, the more I drew clear parallels between the growth of the two enterprises. Clearly, they both disrupted their industry sectors t their advantage.

Foundation for Disruption

Most businesses, business schools and students of business focus on the importance of customers and shareholder value. At Kwik-Fit, Sir Tom saw their people as the key asset above others. They were the ambassadors of the brand, the business and values. "You can't get better than a Kwik-Fit fitter; we're the boys to trust!" was no idle boast.

Their people were well trained for their role and regarded as equals in a democratic company – they had great respect for each other. Secondly, they built genuine partnerships with
suppliers to ensure the quality and range of the products and to assure their higher service levels, the stocks to support the business and the service charter. With these two in place KwikFit would become a household name and attract and retain their customers and finally investors (private and institutional) would be keen to provide funds for development and expansion. This model and its priorities turned the traditional 'tyre and exhaust' business model on its head and gave them a real advantage over others.

Strategic Management and BrewDog

Having just published The Game Changer, admittedly based on what the founders would regard as traditional enterprises or organisations, my initial assumption was that BrewDog might not fit the model and the basis of my experience and my book. Nothing could have been further from the reality.

Here was another dumb assumption on my part – surprisingly the BrewDog founders are well read in management theory, though little is formally practised. They would probably never admit to this, but BrewDog are a living example of what is required of contemporary strategic management – managing strategically in real time, all the time. Their mission, their vision and their values are embedded in their strategies and their people. They set their 'true north' – a central concept in lean manufacturing - and have held that direction since crafting their vision.

They began with a unique vision - mission and purpose - that provided the clear and solid foundation for their enterprise:

"Our brand is not just our identity, it encompasses our entire purpose. People don't just care about either our beer or our PR activity; they buy into our entire entity. Our status as an employer, the values we stand by, our collaborations with other breweries, who we are, and why we are here. To make Punk IPA the best-selling craft beer on the planet. To become the best company to work for... EVER."

They set big, hairy, audacious goals like a corporate value of £1bn by 2020 in 2015 when they barely had enough money to cover the payroll. People are held to account to the 'DOGMAS' - their values that drive performance in a spirit of true empowerment that has eradicated the need for performance reviews. Their founders and leaders lead by example with a restlessness to consign past and current performance to history, as well as being open to their people at all times.

In 2014, BrewDog became the first hospitality company with a national footprint to become a living wage employer. The company also rewards, with a pay rise, everyone who passes the beer professionals' exams run by the US firm Cicerone. (The top grade, Master Cicerone, involves 12 hours
of essays plus a blind tasting of 100 beers; nine people in the world have passed it, and two of them work for BrewDog.)

They set up the Brewdog Academy, initially for the leadership group, for the development of those people who volunteer and demonstrate their passion for personal growth. The company gives 20% of its profits to charities chosen by staff and community as well as its Equity for Punks scheme. Their mission, their vision and their values are embedded in their people and also their stakeholders.

At one with their Community of Stakeholders

From suppliers through customers, partners, equity punks and staff, BrewDog's sense of community shines through with a freshness and positivity seldom found in many enterprises their size. Based adjacent to the heartland of the Scotch Whisky industry in Speyside their location provided access to ingredient sources of the highest quality. Given the challenges facing North East Scotland with the decline of Oil & Gas production and resultant job losses, support from local agencies and councils was assured. This provided the basis for their early growth.

BrewDog's approach to suppliers - an integral part of the community - flew in the face of traditional supply chain design (Michael Porter's Value Chain) by creating a global network that even includes potential competitors. Were they mad? Were they dumb? Far from it. Such was the confidence in the quality and distinctiveness of their products, combined with their passion, this 'co-opetition' became another unique feature of the enterprise.

Attracting people to Ellon, 30 minutes north of Aberdeen, may have presented a challenge for this globally aspiring
business. The challenge may have been less for production or office staff jobs. Attracting more specialist experience in marketing and sales (for example) may have been especially challenging. However, the very distinctiveness and culture of the business would prove to be attractive to many ambitious applicants. The suite of benefits open to all staff is extremely creative and generous as you might expect from BrewDog.

The Equity Punks, those 125,000 investors (over £75m raised to date) inspired by the clarity of vision and passion of the founders have en-abled the establishment of a near global network of breweries, pubs and their unique DogHouse hotels. This feature was not evident in KwikFit who attracted investment from different sources.

1% on Marketing

First impressions would suggest BrewDog must spend heavily on marketing and promotion. The reality is that spend on traditional advertising and marketing is less than 1% of revenue. James Watt's advice on marketing in his 2015 book Business for Punks (Penguin)[1] is revealing. Since these days you *"cannot control your brand, only influence people's perceptions of it"*, Watt writes, *"in today's intercon-nected digital world, full of savvy Gen Y consumers, every single thing you do is marketing."* Allocating a low budget is *"not a problem. In fact, it's a massive advantage."*

Traditional advertising is dead, and in any case unaffordable for a small company *"You'd be better off blow-torching your cash,"* says Watt). Mass media is *"as ignorant as it is irrelevant"*. New media is where it is at. People, Watt writes, *"want genuine, they want quality, they want passionate, they want real, they want integrity"*. He argues, in the modern era, *"The only way to build a brand is to live that brand. You have to live the values and the mission, then let the customer decide."* Their marketing focus is 'product plus community' using social media – without being an expert; just do it. .

Their global expansion has been impressive, especially into the rest of the UK, Europe, the United States and Australia. These represent the most attractive market opportunities for craft beer, with the possible exception of Russia and China – based on consumption/head of population and overall market size.

Power to the People

BrewDog's approach to recruitment unsurprisingly breaks normal conventions. Once again first impressions might be of a wild, beer drinking, revolutionary business. However, they are clearly compliant with employment legislation, though they have positively challenged that legislation on a number of occasions. Their process to bring in new recruits is especially innovative. The 360º hiring process is particularly impressive where they sell the reality to potential recruits and, prior to offer, provide an engagement with future stakeholders e.g. peers, younger members of the team. This provides immediate feedback on potential for followership.

Other than their unique approach to funding and developing the business globally, it is perhaps their approach to leading their people that stands out. The culture is genuinely one of empowered entrepreneurship. Everyone is encouraged to take responsibility for their own performance. As in successful high-performance environments in sport, the 'athletes' set their own bar – the job of the organisation is to challenge and support them to fulfil their ambition
and potential. The culture may sound inspiring but it presents its own challenges. In the early years there was quite a low staff retention rate (<30%), especially from outside the business and its geographic location. Recruitment and retention improved through the expansion of the business in the UK, Europe and globally.

BrewDog and their people just do it, time after time after time. Everyone is held to account to the DOGMAS (the Values that shape the culture). There is a spirit of restlessness (divine discontent with the status quo) that fosters and drives continuous improvement. This would not be achievable without a genuine culture underpinned by empowerment. This requires everyone to be informed and engaged in the business and its performance. Entrepreneurial and energised would be words to describe the culture.

Leaders make frequent use of away-days to discuss openly ways to improve and grow the business. Performance is underpinned by a creative approach to performance assessment. There is no place for the annual appraisal by the boss. Formal performance reviews have been eliminated, replaced by regular one-to-one conversations between employees and their team leaders with an agenda driven by the employee.

High Performing Teams

Team structures are typically cross-departmental and flexible - formed for a mission then often disbanded after achieving their goal. Flexibility is critical because things happen at BrewDog at such a pace that it is impossible to wait until the next plan. A recent example of effective teamwork occurred when crafting a policy for business expenses. As the business grew expenses and spend also grew. Rather than determining a policy created by the HR or Finance department, a cross-functional team was established to come up with the guidelines. Such was the challenge to the culture, the policy ended up as a one-liner – 'spend as if it was your own money'. Not surprisingly expense spend reduced.

In a move reminiscent of Jonathan Ive's (Apple) approach to developing the iPhone the BrewDog Academy was initially set up with volunteers from senior management team who had the desire and ambition to grow and develop. These volunteers drove their own agenda and learning. The Academy meets every second Wednesday where learning and experiences are shared. They choose their own themes/subjects to explore rather than follow a fixed agenda. This process mirrors one of the other business units I have had the pleasure and privilege to work with over the years – M&S's lingerie team – Europe's leading brand who get together most Fridays for a creative 'debrief' of recent experiences and engagements.

Brexit – So Watt?

The negative turmoil around Brexit and the UK's exit from the European Union reached a peak in 2019, just as BrewDog was opening the tap on many new ventures. They were building a brewery in Brisbane, Australia, and plan another in China. The company is opening restaurants in Indianapolis and Cincinnati, and eyeing locations in Shanghai and Kuala Lumpur. They plan to unveil their own Scotch whisky and American whiskey in 2019 – the whisky is maturing while vodka and gin spirits are currently on sale. Brewdog introduced a line of "sour beers" from a new facility at its Scottish base. Watt is betting these fruit-infused brews, which ferment in wine and whiskey barrels instead of stainless-steel tanks, will become the next big thing in the craft beer

craze sweeping the UK and Europe. Watt and Dickie
and their leadership team have been developing several plans for dealing with a hard Brexit, from asking European partners to temporarily share brewing capacity to building a plant in a EU nation. They also contemplate shipping beer from BrewDog's two-year-old U.S. brewery in Columbus, Ohio. 2019 also saw the acquisition of a brewery in Berlin (pictured below).

Watt shrugs off such concerns. "We're not too worried about demand if it's something we're passionate about," he says. "Our business plan has always been death or glory." He and Dickie have taken that 'devil may care' attitude ever since they started brewing beer in 2007, inspired by the hoppy pale ales of California.

"It's been a crazy first 10 years. Here's to the next 10!"

The BrewDog Blueprint

2018 saw the launch of The BrewDog BluePrint – their vision for the next 10 years.

In the first ten years, spurred by their passion, mission and community they have gone from two humans and a dog to a vibrant purpose-driven business, with over 1,000 team members. They are no longer a small, inconsequential company in a beer industry dominated by the major brewers (their largest competitor is over 2,500 times their size).

The founders are determined to show that craft beer can be a force for good in the world, and build a completely new type of business. They have done some amazing things, taken some insane risks and always worn their hearts on their sleeves.

Their divine discontent will always drive them to improve, to get better and work towards their goals continuously. Their published aim in Blue-Print 2018 is to focus less on crazy growth and even more on crafting the best business and the best beers they possibly can.

As a company the things they care most about are BrewDog's beer, their people and the business mission. The first ten years have provided a unique platform, an opportunity to invest even more into their beers and their people, and an opportunity to continue building a completely new type of business.

They remain determined to continue making a stand for independence; a stand for quality and a stand for craft. Alongside their Equity Punks and incredible team, they aim to make a meaningful impact on both the world of beer and the world of business.

"At BrewDog, we are determined to show that craft beer can be a force for good in the world, and build a completely new type of business. A business that is part community owned, a business that gives back, a business that is open and transparent and a business that looks after its people incredibly well."

The BrewDog Blueprint 2018

4. Brewdog - The Real Game Changer

*H*aving just published *The Game Changer*, admittedly based on what the BrewDog founders might regard as traditional enterprises or organisations, I believed BrewDog would fit the model that is the basis of the book.

The previous two chapters provide evidence of that position. In this chapter I summarise what lies behind BrewDog's game-changing status in strategic management – in real time, all the time.

Their strategy is clear in comparison to the major brewers:

UK Beer Industry	BrewDog (Craft Beer)
• Low margin, high volume	• Sustain margins
• High cost of entry	• Low cost of entry
• Price focused	• High quality
• Profit motive	• Passion and mission
• Declining annual growth	• High growth (+30% annual)

But Does BrewDog display the features of The Game Changer?

The Game Changer is based on how organisations in business, sport, the public sector and not-for profit organisations not only improved performance in the long-term, they changed the rules of the game.

Five features emerge that when executed enabled the organisations to secure sustainable performance.

The Game Changers:

1. Broke the rules - challenged existing paradigms and business models

2. Worked it out themselves – embraced change management

3. Planned for a step-change in performance

4. Change organisational performance

5. Leaders at all levels in the organisations championed the change.

The real and dominant difference is the Game Changers did all of these features **at the same time** in a game-changing project or initiative rather than cherry picking fads or tools they felt comfortable with.

The Game Changer organisations believe in making 'Love not War'. Conventionally, all of the major frameworks of strategy start by assuming that the essence of strategy is to achieve superior competitive advantage. I believe this as a concept, and more importantly mindset, is extremely out of date and dangerous, because it puts competitors firmly at centre stage. In doing so there is the tendency to watch competitors and try to imitate them. Recent examples from the banking and utilities industries would reinforce this view.

Imitation creates sameness. Sameness will never bring greatness and the final result is something that is often the worst thing that can happen to a business – becoming a . commodity. You need look no further than the volume beer businesses to see this in action. Commodity strategies are often the outcome of the same or similar people, with the same qualifications, in the same environment supported by the same consultants - coming up with the same strategies. Commodity strategy means no differentiation in your product or service and consequently all you can do is fight on price, rather than commanding a premium – the true outcome of real differentiation. The consequence is aggressive rivalry. In order to win you have to defeat someone else. It is the strategy of war, with many military analogies being used to determine what is a 'good' strategy.

If competitors are not at the centre of strategic thinking, then who is? The answer is obvious. The customer. The customer is the focal point and the driving force for strategy. The key is to develop a deep understanding of customer requirements and how you can help your customer in the most effective way. So rather than imitate a competitor, you separate yourself from the pack by producing something of value that is unique, that adds value to the customer and expresses real passion, care and concern for the customer. Value comes from mutual trust and respect, mutual benefits, transparency of transactions and a genuine and strong relationship between people in the organisations. Strategy is more about love than war.

The previous chapter illustrated the rapid growth enjoyed by BrewDog, especially in the last 5 years. When I was with PA Technology [2]we researched the phenomenon of high-growth companies to identify the features of these organisations.

We found the high-growth companies focused on:

1. Playing in a strong, well defined niche

2. Geographical growth, rather than eking out the last percentage point of market share in the home market

3. Emphasis on speed of response, rather than cost

4. Adding value to existing concepts

5. Being responsive to market needs.

Once again BrewDog ticks the boxes here.

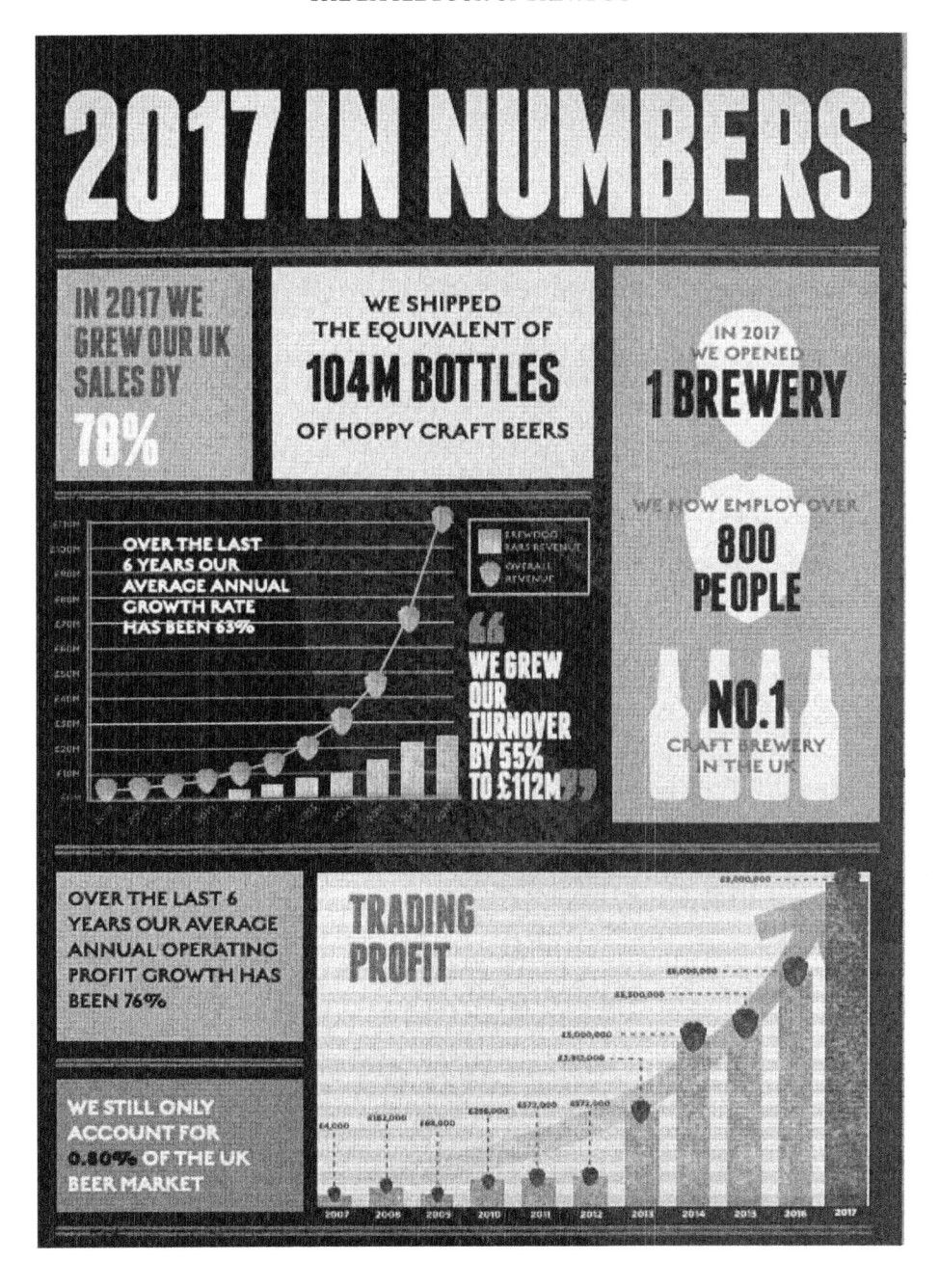

2018 Trading Results reflect further growth increased Investment
BrewDog increased sales by 55% in 2018 to £172m driven by organic growth and acquisitions, with EBITDA[3] at £8.3m marginally down on 2017's £8.9m. Overheads increased by 60% driven by recruitment of key executives, marketing, the increasing bar network in the UK and overseas. BrewDog continues to generate strong underlying profits and cash flows. Net assets increased by 14% to £165m.

BrewDog operates more than 80 bars globally, places where customers can in indulge in everything that is great about craft beer. Their staff are knowledgable and passionately evangelical when it comes to craft beers. The bars serve as key focal points in the craft beer revolution as they continue their mission to share the passion they have for everything craft beer.

The Love of the Punks
The Equity Punks care most about BrewDog's beer, people and their mission. The first ten years have provided a unique platform, an opportunity to invest even more into their beers and their people and an opportunity to continue building a completely new type of business. They remain determined to continue making a stand for independence, a stand for quality and a stand for craft. Alongside their Equity Punks and incredible team they aim to make a meaningful impact on both the world of beer and the world of business.In January 2020 they launched BrewDog Tomorrow. BrewDog Tomorrow is a further commitment to combine brave thinking and bold action to help ensure the world has a planet to produce beer for **future** generations. BrewDog may have matured (a bit) but the 'underdog' spirit is alive and well. They are determined to continuously raise the bar and set a new standard for beer and business..

Since commencing my quest to understand what lies behind their success I have heard from a number of individuals who left the 'comfort' of major brewers and distillers to join BrewDog. Many did not last long - surely not surprising given the embedded culture they left behind in the establishment.

The culture of the entrepreneurial organisation is never going to be a safe haven for the graduate of the established brewers and distillers. They continually seek major business processes or systematic solutions above building a values-driven culture linked to the founders' divine discontent with the status quo.

To Conclude

So how does BrewDog change the game through their leadership and management of the enterprise? The summary conclusions follow:

How BrewDog changed the Game

- **Broke the Rules** – challenged existing Paradigms
  - Revolution over commercial mediocrity
  - Global, not local
  - Part Community-owned – crowdfunding - Equity for Punks
  - Gonzo marketing
  - Partnerships with competitors
- **Worked it out Themselves** – embraced Change Management
  - Engagement of the whole organisation in the Vision
  - Divine discontent – fostering culture never to be satisfied with the current performance
  - 'Be happy be scrappy' – no gloss; the bigger we get the smaller we have to think.
- **Planned for a Step-Change in Performance**
  - Big goals for 2020 – valued at $1bn
  - Global vision – implemented locally in the most attractive global markets, where they had potential advantage
- **Changed Organisational Performance**
  - Empowered entrepreneurs led by the founders and their executive
  - Flexible use of teams with a mission to improve; often cross- functional
  - Spend, as if it were your own money
- **Leaders at all Levels in the organisation championed the Change**
  - Leaders open to their people with genuine Followership
  - Everyone an empowered entrepreneur – eradicated formal performance reviews
  - The DOGMAS – breeding with courage and passion
  - The BrewDog Academy – commitment to learning and development.

It has been both a privilege and a pleasure to research and analyse the performance of BrewDog, during their brief and spectacular history. It is often dangerous to fit a particular organisation into a business model or paradigm to claim some special insight. In this case I am sure the founders and their community of employees, equity punks, loyal customers and other stakeholders will keep challenging any conclusive research to build yet another game-changing paradigm.

As a modest shareholder and Equity Punk I would simply conclude by reflecting the words of the founders - the true Game Changers:

"At BrewDog, we are determined to show that craft beer can be a force for good in the world and build a completely new type of business. A business that is part-community-owned; a business that gives back; a business that is open and transparent and a business that looks after its people incredibly well. It's been a crazy first 10 years. Here's to the next 10!"

The BrewDog Blueprint 2018

5. Acknowledgements

People

The inspiration for The BrewDog trilogy emerged from work I carried out for Opportunity North East in 2019.

Opportunity North East was launched in December 2015, following extensive consultation with the region's business community and discussion with the public sector. It is the private sector's response to the special economic challenges in the region, especially in light of the potentially negative impact of the decline of the oil and gas exploration industry.

I had the privilege to work with their Chief Executive, Jennifer Craw and her Deputy, Maggie McGinlay to facilitate 4 sector board session sand a special one with their main board, chaired by Sir Ian Wood. The aim was to create a vision of success for the region in the sectors that would underpin the region into the future. They include food & drink, tourism, energy transition, life science and digital.

I would like to express my special thanks to Lisa Paton, David Mac-Dowall and Nicolle Sinclair, all great BrewDog people, for giving me special insight into their great enterprise.

Just as with The Game Changer I am indebted to Sheila, my wife, who did the hard-yards reading successive proofs and making a number of helpful suggestions.

Images and Charts:

I acknowledge that the source for all images and charts are on the

BrewDog website (www.brewdog.com) or from published information e,g, BrewDog Annual Reports and publications e.g Blueprint 2018.

6. The Game Changer

Published by Routledge in 2019 (ISBN: ISBN 978113836272), THE GAME CHANGER outlines how a number of organisations in business and sport have done more than raise their performance. They have also changed the rules of the game in their industry.

These organisations were all clients of Genesis, the consulting firm established by Alistair Gray in 1992. Each of 20 chapters includes a themed article on an area of strategic management and a case study, along with a summary as to how they 'changed the game'.

Throughout this book there are real examples of client projects that bring theory and process to life, with positive outcomes. Many of the clients secured significantly improved strategic outcomes and higher levels of performance from their people.

Foreword by Sir Tom Farmer, KBE Founder of Kwik-Fit.

Endorsements of The Game Changer

"Altogether, The Game Changer is a really useful book whose articles and case studies will be invaluable for anyone facing the prospect of competing in the challenging global markets of the 21st century."

Sir Tom Farmer, KBE, Founder of KwikFit

"The Game Changer is a source of useful learning for MBA students and young executives. Alistair delivers a unique perspective on many aspects of strategic management supported by real life case studies from business and sport. I have taken benefit from Alistair and his approach to accelerate the University's strategy."
Professor Sir Jim McDonald, Principal and Vice Chancellor, University of Strathclyde

"Alistair Gray has a lifetime of experience in business and sport and his books provide an insight into the strategic management, innovation and drivers needed to change the game"
Baroness Sue Campbell CBE, Director of Women's Football at The FA. Chair of UK Sport (2003 – 2013) and Youth Sport Trust (2005 – 2017)

"The Game Changer is a very enlightening and well researched read from a wise sage who knows - from first-hand experience - more than a bit about what provides the zeitgeist in business".
Andy Nash, Portfolio Chair and former Director of Taunton Cider PLC

"A supportive infrastructure is key to ensuring coaches and other performance specialists in sport can exercise their skills effectively. Alistair applies his unique skills set to creating such infrastructure by tackling culture shift head on. Putting it another way, he facilitates performance excellence."
Professor Frank Dick OBE, Coach and Motivational Speaker

"It is one thing to write about strategy and how it should be done. It is a completely different thing to write about strategy and to have actually done it. Alistair Gray provides the latter in his book. It is a tremendous read packed with insight how to deliver meaningful strategic change."
Harry Sminea, Professor of Strategic Management, Strathclyde Business School, University of Strathclyde

"Top business frequently turns to sport for strategies to improve performance. Alistair Gray benefits from his unique combination of a successful voluntary leader in sport and respected consultant to leading businesses and sports around the world. The Game Changer and this case study deliver real insight into how to succeed."
Martin Gilbert, Former Joint CEO of Standard Life Aberdeen PLC

---

[1] Business for Punks, James Watt; Penguin Random House 2016 (ISBN 978-0-241-29011-8)

[2] High Growth Companies – Driving the Tiger by Thomas Ahrens; Gower Publishing Co; Subsequent Edition (March 1, 1999)

[3] EBITDA – Earnings before interest, taxes, depreciation and amortisation is used as a proxy for a business's current operating profitability.

Printed in Great Britain
by Amazon